How To Be A Better Restaurant Server

Learning to Better Myself as a Server
To Make Me Better At My Job!

This book will help you learn how to be more
efficient on a daily to weekly basis.

Sharon Hicks

For information, contact
Sharon Hicks @

shyksos@gmail.com

Dedication

To my Daughter who works as a server.

My Place of Employment

Name of Restaurant _____

Head Waiter _____

Immediate Supervisor _____

Person Who Trained Me _____

Date I Started _____

Starting Wage _____

This Book Belongs To _____

My Work Phone Number Is _____

My Work Address Is _____

How to use this Workbook

Waiting tables is challenging. So much to do, so much to remember.

Use this workbook to help improve your serving techniques.

It includes spaces for you to:

Keep track of your own performance of how you treated your customers.

How fast you learned your duties.

Answer the questions in this book

Then write down your own thoughts

How do I make them glad they came?

This is the first step to a good meal for your customers!

Did the customer come in with a smile?_____

Did I greet my customers with a smile? _____

Did I give them their menu(s) when I seated them? _____

Were the specials discussed? _____

If yes, could I repeat them without looking?_____

Did I get their order correct? _____

Why or Why Not?_____

Did I check for condiments when I took their order?_____

How often and how many times did I stop at each table?_____

Were unnecessary trips made because I forgot something?
_____

Did I have to have help with my tables? _____ Why? _____
_____

Was I kind and courteous at all times?_____
_____

Did the customers leave with a smile?_____

What could I do differently?_____
_____

How I made them glad they came!

What did I learn today? _____

_____

How can I apply it tomorrow? _____

_____

What did I learn yesterday?_____

_____

Did I apply that today? _____

Who taught me something new today?_____

_____

Am I doing better than when I started?_____

_____

My Thoughts:

_____

_____

_____

_____

_____

_____

How do I make them glad they came?

Date _____

This is the first step to a good meal for your customers!

Did the customer come in with a smile?_____

Did I greet my customers with a smile? _____

Did I give them their menu(s) when I seated them?
_____

Were the specials discussed? _____

If yes, could I repeat them without looking? _____

Did I get their order correct? _____

Why or Why Not?_____

Did I check for condiments when I took their order?_____

How often and how many times did I stop at each table?_____

Were unnecessary trips made because I forgot something?

_____

Did I have to have help with my tables? _____ Why? _____

_____

Was I kind and courteous at all times?_____

_____

Did the customers leave with a smile?_____

What could I do differently?_____

_____

How I made them glad they came!

What did I learn today? _____

_____

How can I apply it tomorrow? _____

_____

What did I learn yesterday? _____

_____

Did I apply that today? _____

Who taught me something new today? _____

_____

Am I doing better than when I started? _____

_____

My Thoughts:

_____

_____

_____

_____

_____

_____

How do I make them glad they came?

Date _____

This is the first step to a good meal for your customers!

Did the customer come in with a smile?_____

Did I greet my customers with a smile? _____

Did I give them their menu(s) when I seated them?
_____

Were the specials discussed? _____

If yes, could I repeat them without looking? _____

Did I get their order correct? _____

Why or Why Not?_____

Did I check for condiments when I took their order?_____

How often and how many times did I stop at each table?_____

Were unnecessary trips made because I forgot something?

_____

Did I have to have help with my tables? _____ Why? _____

_____

Was I kind and courteous at all times?_____

_____

Did the customers leave with a smile?_____

What could I do differently?_____

_____

How I made them glad they came!

What did I learn today? _____

_____

How can I apply it tomorrow? _____

_____

What did I learn yesterday? _____

_____

Did I apply that today? _____

Who taught me something new today? _____

_____

Am I doing better than when I started? _____

_____

My Thoughts:

_____

_____

_____

_____

_____

_____

How do I make them glad they came?

Date _____

This is the first step to a good meal for your customers!

Did the customer come in with a smile?_____

Did I greet my customers with a smile? _____

Did I give them their menu(s) when I seated them?
_____

Were the specials discussed? _____

If yes, could I repeat them without looking? _____

Did I get their order correct? _____

Why or Why Not?_____

Did I check for condiments when I took their order?_____

How often and how many times did I stop at each table?_____

Were unnecessary trips made because I forgot something?
_____

Did I have to have help with my tables? _____ Why? _____
_____

Was I kind and courteous at all times?_____
_____

Did the customers leave with a smile?_____

What could I do differently?_____

_____

How I made them glad they came!

What did I learn today? _____

_____

How can I apply it tomorrow? _____

_____

What did I learn yesterday?_____

_____

Did I apply that today? _____

Who taught me something new today?_____

_____

Am I doing better than when I started?_____

_____

My Thoughts:

_____

_____

_____

_____

_____

_____

How do I make them glad they came?

Date _____

This is the first step to a good meal for your customers!

Did the customer come in with a smile?_____

Did I greet my customers with a smile? _____

Did I give them their menu(s) when I seated them? _____

Were the specials discussed? _____

If yes, could I repeat them without looking? _____

Did I get their order correct? _____

Why or Why Not?_____

Did I check for condiments when I took their order?_____

How often and how many times did I stop at each table?_____

Were unnecessary trips made because I forgot something?

_____

Did I have to have help with my tables? _____ Why? _____

_____

Was I kind and courteous at all times?_____

_____

Did the customers leave with a smile?_____

What could I do differently?_____

_____

How I made them glad they came!

What did I learn today? _____

_____

How can I apply it tomorrow? _____

_____

What did I learn yesterday?_____

_____

Did I apply that today? _____

Who taught me something new today?_____

_____

Am I doing better than when I started?_____

_____

My Thoughts:

_____

_____

_____

_____

_____

_____

How do I make them glad they came?

Date _____

This is the first step to a good meal for your customers!

Did the customer come in with a smile?_____

Did I greet my customers with a smile? _____

Did I give them their menu(s) when I seated them?
_____

Were the specials discussed? _____

If yes, could I repeat them without looking?_____

Did I get their order correct? _____

Why or Why Not?_____

Did I check for condiments when I took their order?_____

How often and how many times did I stop at each table?_____

Were unnecessary trips made because I forgot something?
_____

Did I have to have help with my tables? _____ Why? _____
_____

Was I kind and courteous at all times?_____
_____

Did the customers leave with a smile?_____

What could I do differently?_____

_____

How I made them glad they came!

What did I learn today? _____

_____

How can I apply it tomorrow? _____

_____

What did I learn yesterday?_____

_____

Did I apply that today? _____

Who taught me something new today?_____

_____

Am I doing better than when I started?_____

_____

My Thoughts:

_____

_____

_____

_____

_____

_____

How do I make them glad they came?

This is the first step to a good meal for your customers!

Did the customer come in with a smile?_____

Did I greet my customers with a smile? _____

Did I give them their menu(s) when I seated them?
_____

Were the specials discussed? _____

If yes, could I repeat them without looking? _____

Did I get their order correct? _____

Why or Why Not?_____

Did I check for condiments when I took their order?_____

How often and how many times did I stop at each table?_____

Were unnecessary trips made because I forgot something?
_____

Did I have to have help with my tables? _____ Why? _____
_____

Was I kind and courteous at all times?_____
_____

Did the customers leave with a smile?_____

What could I do differently?_____

_____

How I made them glad they came!

What did I learn today? _____
_____

How can I apply it tomorrow? _____
_____

What did I learn yesterday?_____

_____

Did I apply that today? _____

Who taught me something new today?_____
_____

Am I doing better than when I started?_____

_____

My Thoughts:

_____

_____

_____

_____

_____

_____

How do I make them glad they came?

This is the first step to a good meal for your customers!

Did the customer come in with a smile?_____

Did I greet my customers with a smile? _____

Did I give them their menu(s) when I seated them?
_____

Were the specials discussed? _____

If yes, could I repeat them without looking? _____

Did I get their order correct? _____

Why or Why Not?_____

Did I check for condiments when I took their order?_____

How often and how many times did I stop at each table?_____

Were unnecessary trips made because I forgot something?

_____

Did I have to have help with my tables? _____ Why? _____

_____

Was I kind and courteous at all times?_____

_____

Did the customers leave with a smile?_____

What could I do differently?_____

_____

How I made them glad they came!

What did I learn today? _____

_____

How can I apply it tomorrow? _____

_____

What did I learn yesterday?_____

_____

Did I apply that today? _____

Who taught me something new today?_____

_____

Am I doing better than when I started?_____

_____

My Thoughts:

_____

_____

_____

_____

_____

How do I make them glad they came?

Date _____

This is the first step to a good meal for your customers!

Did the customer come in with a smile?_____

Did I greet my customers with a smile? _____

Did I give them their menu(s) when I seated them?
_____

Were the specials discussed? _____

If yes, could I repeat them without looking? _____

Did I get their order correct? _____

Why or Why Not?_____

Did I check for condiments when I took their order?_____

How often and how many times did I stop at each table?_____

Were unnecessary trips made because I forgot something?
_____

Did I have to have help with my tables? _____ Why? _____
_____

Was I kind and courteous at all times?_____
_____

Did the customers leave with a smile?_____

What could I do differently?_____

_____

How I made them glad they came!

What did I learn today? _____

_____

How can I apply it tomorrow? _____

_____

What did I learn yesterday?_____

_____

Did I apply that today? _____

Who taught me something new today?_____

_____

Am I doing better than when I started?_____

_____

My Thoughts:

_____

_____

_____

_____

_____

How do I make them glad they came?

This is the first step to a good meal for your customers!

Did the customer come in with a smile?_____

Did I greet my customers with a smile? _____

Did I give them their menu(s) when I seated them?
_____

Were the specials discussed? _____

If yes, could I repeat them without looking? _____

Did I get their order correct? _____

Why or Why Not?_____

Did I check for condiments when I took their order?_____

How often and how many times did I stop at each table?_____

Were unnecessary trips made because I forgot something?
_____

Did I have to have help with my tables? _____ Why? _____
_____

Was I kind and courteous at all times?_____
_____

Did the customers leave with a smile?_____

What could I do differently?_____

_____

How I made them glad they came!

What did I learn today? _____

_____

How can I apply it tomorrow? _____

_____

What did I learn yesterday?_____

_____

Did I apply that today? _____

Who taught me something new today?_____

_____

Am I doing better than when I started?_____

_____

My Thoughts:

_____

_____

_____

_____

_____

How do I make them glad they came?

Date _____

This is the first step to a good meal for your customers!

Did the customer come in with a smile?_____

Did I greet my customers with a smile? _____

Did I give them their menu(s) when I seated them? _____

Were the specials discussed? _____

If yes, could I repeat them without looking? _____

Did I get their order correct? _____

Why or Why Not?_____

Did I check for condiments when I took their order?_____

How often and how many times did I stop at each table?_____

Were unnecessary trips made because I forgot something?

_____

Did I have to have help with my tables? _____ Why? _____

_____

Was I kind and courteous at all times?_____

_____

Did the customers leave with a smile?_____

What could I do differently?_____

_____

How I made them glad they came!

What did I learn today? _____

_____

How can I apply it tomorrow? _____

_____

What did I learn yesterday? _____

_____

Did I apply that today? _____

Who taught me something new today? _____

_____

Am I doing better than when I started? _____

_____

My Thoughts:

_____

_____

_____

_____

_____

_____

How do I make them glad they came?

Date _____

This is the first step to a good meal for your customers!

Did the customer come in with a smile?_____

Did I greet my customers with a smile? _____

Did I give them their menu(s) when I seated them? _____

Were the specials discussed? _____

If yes, could I repeat them without looking? _____

Did I get their order correct? _____

Why or Why Not?_____

Did I check for condiments when I took their order?_____

How often and how many times did I stop at each table?_____

Were unnecessary trips made because I forgot something?

_____

Did I have to have help with my tables? _____ Why? _____

_____

Was I kind and courteous at all times?_____

_____

Did the customers leave with a smile?_____

What could I do differently?_____

_____

How I made them glad they came!

What did I learn today? _____

_____

How can I apply it tomorrow? _____

_____

What did I learn yesterday?_____

_____

Did I apply that today? _____

Who taught me something new today?_____

_____

Am I doing better than when I started?_____

_____

My Thoughts:

_____

_____

_____

_____

_____

_____

How do I make them glad they came?

This is the first step to a good meal for your customers!

Did the customer come in with a smile?_____

Did I greet my customers with a smile? _____

Did I give them their menu(s) when I seated them?
_____

Were the specials discussed? _____

If yes, could I repeat them without looking? _____

Did I get their order correct? _____

Why or Why Not?_____

Did I check for condiments when I took their order?_____

How often and how many times did I stop at each table?_____

Were unnecessary trips made because I forgot something?

_____

Did I have to have help with my tables? _____ Why? _____

_____

Was I kind and courteous at all times?_____

_____

Did the customers leave with a smile?_____

What could I do differently?_____

_____

How I made them glad they came!

What did I learn today? _____

_____

How can I apply it tomorrow? _____

_____

What did I learn yesterday?_____

_____

Did I apply that today? _____

Who taught me something new today?_____

_____

Am I doing better than when I started?_____

_____

My Thoughts:

_____

_____

_____

_____

_____

How do I make them glad they came?

Date _____

This is the first step to a good meal for your customers!

Did the customer come in with a smile?_____

Did I greet my customers with a smile? _____

Did I give them their menu(s) when I seated them?
_____

Were the specials discussed? _____

If yes, could I repeat them without looking? _____

Did I get their order correct? _____

Why or Why Not?_____

Did I check for condiments when I took their order?_____

How often and how many times did I stop at each table?_____

Were unnecessary trips made because I forgot something?

_____

Did I have to have help with my tables? _____ Why? _____

_____

Was I kind and courteous at all times?_____

_____

Did the customers leave with a smile?_____

What could I do differently?_____

_____

How I made them glad they came!

What did I learn today? _____

_____

How can I apply it tomorrow? _____

_____

What did I learn yesterday?_____

_____

Did I apply that today? _____

Who taught me something new today?_____

_____

Am I doing better than when I started?_____

_____

My Thoughts:

_____

_____

_____

_____

_____

_____

How do I make them glad they came?

Date _____

This is the first step to a good meal for your customers!

Did the customer come in with a smile?_____

Did I greet my customers with a smile? _____

Did I give them their menu(s) when I seated them?
_____

Were the specials discussed? _____

If yes, could I repeat them without looking? _____

Did I get their order correct? _____

Why or Why Not?_____

Did I check for condiments when I took their order?_____

How often and how many times did I stop at each table?_____

Were unnecessary trips made because I forgot something?
_____

Did I have to have help with my tables? _____ Why? _____
_____

Was I kind and courteous at all times?_____
_____

Did the customers leave with a smile?_____

What could I do differently?_____
_____

How I made them glad they came!

What did I learn today? _____

_____

How can I apply it tomorrow? _____

_____

What did I learn yesterday? _____

_____

Did I apply that today? _____

Who taught me something new today? _____

_____

Am I doing better than when I started? _____

_____

My Thoughts:

_____

_____

_____

_____

_____

_____

How do I make them glad they came?

This is the first step to a good meal for your customers!

Did the customer come in with a smile?_____

Did I greet my customers with a smile? _____

Did I give them their menu(s) when I seated them?
_____

Were the specials discussed? _____

If yes, could I repeat them without looking? _____

Did I get their order correct? _____

Why or Why Not?_____

Did I check for condiments when I took their order?_____

How often and how many times did I stop at each table?_____

Were unnecessary trips made because I forgot something?
_____

Did I have to have help with my tables? _____ Why? _____
_____

Was I kind and courteous at all times?_____
_____

Did the customers leave with a smile?_____

What could I do differently?_____
_____

How I made them glad they came!

What did I learn today? _____

_____

How can I apply it tomorrow? _____

_____

What did I learn yesterday?_____

_____

Did I apply that today? _____

Who taught me something new today?_____

_____

Am I doing better than when I started?_____

_____

My Thoughts:

_____

_____

_____

_____

_____

How do I make them glad they came?

Date _____

This is the first step to a good meal for your customers!

Did the customer come in with a smile?_____

Did I greet my customers with a smile? _____

Did I give them their menu(s) when I seated them? _____

Were the specials discussed? _____

If yes, could I repeat them without looking?_____

Did I get their order correct? _____

Why or Why Not?_____

Did I check for condiments when I took their order?_____

How often and how many times did I stop at each table?_____

Were unnecessary trips made because I forgot something?

_____

Did I have to have help with my tables? _____ Why? _____

_____

Was I kind and courteous at all times?_____

_____

Did the customers leave with a smile?_____

What could I do differently?_____

_____

How I made them glad they came!

What did I learn today? _____

_____

How can I apply it tomorrow? _____

_____

What did I learn yesterday?_____

_____

Did I apply that today? _____

Who taught me something new today? _____

_____

Am I doing better than when I started?_____

_____

My Thoughts:

_____

_____

_____

_____

_____

_____

How do I make them glad they came?

Date _____

This is the first step to a good meal for your customers!

Did the customer come in with a smile?_____

Did I greet my customers with a smile? _____

Did I give them their menu(s) when I seated them?
_____

Were the specials discussed? _____

If yes, could I repeat them without looking?_____

Did I get their order correct? _____

Why or Why Not?_____

Did I check for condiments when I took their order?_____

How often and how many times did I stop at each table?_____

Were unnecessary trips made because I forgot something?
_____

Did I have to have help with my tables? _____ Why? _____
_____

Was I kind and courteous at all times?_____
_____

Did the customers leave with a smile?_____

What could I do differently?_____

_____

How I made them glad they came!

What did I learn today? _____

_____

How can I apply it tomorrow? _____

_____

What did I learn yesterday?_____

_____

Did I apply that today? _____

Who taught me something new today?_____

_____

Am I doing better than when I started?_____

_____

My Thoughts:

_____

_____

_____

_____

_____

How do I make them glad they came?

Date _____

This is the first step to a good meal for your customers!

Did the customer come in with a smile?_____

Did I greet my customers with a smile? _____

Did I give them their menu(s) when I seated them?
_____

Were the specials discussed? _____

If yes, could I repeat them without looking?_____

Did I get their order correct? _____

Why or Why Not?_____

Did I check for condiments when I took their order?_____

How often and how many times did I stop at each table?_____

Were unnecessary trips made because I forgot something?
_____

Did I have to have help with my tables? _____ Why? _____
_____

Was I kind and courteous at all times?_____
_____

Did the customers leave with a smile?_____

What could I do differently?_____

_____

How do I make them glad they came?

Date _____

This is the first step to a good meal for your customers!

Did the customer come in with a smile?_____

Did I greet my customers with a smile? _____

Did I give them their menu(s) when I seated them?
_____

Were the specials discussed? _____

If yes, could I repeat them without looking? _____

Did I get their order correct? _____

Why or Why Not?_____

Did I check for condiments when I took their order?_____

How often and how many times did I stop at each table?_____

Were unnecessary trips made because I forgot something?

_____

Did I have to have help with my tables? _____ Why? _____

_____

Was I kind and courteous at all times?_____

_____

Did the customers leave with a smile?_____

What could I do differently?_____

_____

How I made them glad they came!

What did I learn today? _____

_____

How can I apply it tomorrow? _____

_____

What did I learn yesterday?_____

_____

Did I apply that today? _____

Who taught me something new today?_____

_____

Am I doing better than when I started?_____

_____

My Thoughts:

_____

_____

_____

_____

_____

_____

How do I make them glad they came?

Date _____

This is the first step to a good meal for your customers!

Did the customer come in with a smile?_____

Did I greet my customers with a smile? _____

Did I give them their menu(s) when I seated them? _____

Were the specials discussed? _____

If yes, could I repeat them without looking?_____

Did I get their order correct? _____

Why or Why Not?_____

Did I check for condiments when I took their order?_____

How often and how many times did I stop at each table?_____

Were unnecessary trips made because I forgot something?

_____

Did I have to have help with my tables? _____ Why? _____

_____

Was I kind and courteous at all times?_____

_____

Did the customers leave with a smile?_____

What could I do differently?_____

_____

How I made them glad they came!

What did I learn today? _____

_____

How can I apply it tomorrow? _____

_____

What did I learn yesterday?_____

_____

Did I apply that today? _____

Who taught me something new today?_____

_____

Am I doing better than when I started?_____

_____

My Thoughts:

_____

_____

_____

_____

_____

How do I make them glad they came?

Date _____

This is the first step to a good meal for your customers!

Did the customer come in with a smile?_____

Did I greet my customers with a smile? _____

Did I give them their menu(s) when I seated them? _____

Were the specials discussed? _____

If yes, could I repeat them without looking?_____

Did I get their order correct? _____

Why or Why Not?_____

Did I check for condiments when I took their order?_____

How often and how many times did I stop at each table?_____

Were unnecessary trips made because I forgot something?

_____

Did I have to have help with my tables? _____ Why? _____

_____

Was I kind and courteous at all times?_____

_____

Did the customers leave with a smile?_____

What could I do differently?_____

_____

How I made them glad they came!

What did I learn today? _____

_____

How can I apply it tomorrow? _____

_____

What did I learn yesterday? _____

_____

Did I apply that today? _____

Who taught me something new today? _____

_____

Am I doing better than when I started? _____

_____

My Thoughts:

_____

_____

_____

_____

_____

How do I make them glad they came?

Date _____

This is the first step to a good meal for your customers!

Did the customer come in with a smile?_____

Did I greet my customers with a smile? _____

Did I give them their menu(s) when I seated them?
_____

Were the specials discussed? _____

If yes, could I repeat them without looking? _____

Did I get their order correct? _____

Why or Why Not?_____

Did I check for condiments when I took their order?_____

How often and how many times did I stop at each table?_____

Were unnecessary trips made because I forgot something?
_____

Did I have to have help with my tables? _____ Why? _____
_____

Was I kind and courteous at all times?_____
_____

Did the customers leave with a smile?_____

What could I do differently?_____

_____

How I made them glad they came!

What did I learn today? _____

_____

How can I apply it tomorrow? _____

_____

What did I learn yesterday?_____

_____

Did I apply that today? _____

Who taught me something new today?_____

_____

Am I doing better than when I started?_____

_____

My Thoughts:

_____

_____

_____

_____

_____

_____

How do I make them glad they came?

Date _____

This is the first step to a good meal for your customers!

Did the customer come in with a smile?_____

Did I greet my customers with a smile? _____

Did I give them their menu(s) when I seated them? _____

Were the specials discussed? _____

If yes, could I repeat them without looking?_____

Did I get their order correct? _____

Why or Why Not?_____

Did I check for condiments when I took their order?_____

How often and how many times did I stop at each table?_____

Were unnecessary trips made because I forgot something?

_____

Did I have to have help with my tables? _____ Why? _____

_____

Was I kind and courteous at all times?_____

_____

Did the customers leave with a smile?_____

What could I do differently?_____

_____

How I made them glad they came!

What did I learn today? _____

_____

How can I apply it tomorrow? _____

_____

What did I learn yesterday?_____

_____

Did I apply that today? _____

Who taught me something new today?_____

_____

Am I doing better than when I started?_____

_____

My Thoughts:

_____

_____

_____

_____

_____

_____

How do I make them glad they came?

Date _____

This is the first step to a good meal for your customers!

Did the customer come in with a smile?_____

Did I greet my customers with a smile? _____

Did I give them their menu(s) when I seated them? _____

Were the specials discussed? _____

If yes, could I repeat them without looking? _____

Did I get their order correct? _____

Why or Why Not?_____

Did I check for condiments when I took their order?_____

How often and how many times did I stop at each table?_____

Were unnecessary trips made because I forgot something?

_____

Did I have to have help with my tables? _____ Why? _____

_____

Was I kind and courteous at all times?_____

_____

Did the customers leave with a smile?_____

What could I do differently?_____

_____

How I made them glad they came!

What did I learn today? _____

_____

How can I apply it tomorrow? _____

_____

What did I learn yesterday?_____

_____

Did I apply that today? _____

Who taught me something new today?_____

_____

Am I doing better than when I started?_____

_____

My Thoughts:

_____

_____

_____

_____

_____

_____

How do I make them glad they came?

Date _____

This is the first step to a good meal for your customers!

Did the customer come in with a smile?_____

Did I greet my customers with a smile? _____

Did I give them their menu(s) when I seated them?
_____

Were the specials discussed? _____

If yes, could I repeat them without looking?_____

Did I get their order correct? _____

Why or Why Not?_____

Did I check for condiments when I took their order?_____

How often and how many times did I stop at each table?_____

Were unnecessary trips made because I forgot something?
_____

Did I have to have help with my tables? _____ Why? _____
_____

Was I kind and courteous at all times?_____
_____

Did the customers leave with a smile?_____

What could I do differently?_____

_____

How I made them glad they came!

What did I learn today? _____

_____

How can I apply it tomorrow? _____

_____

What did I learn yesterday?_____

_____

Did I apply that today? _____

Who taught me something new today?_____

_____

Am I doing better than when I started?_____

_____

My Thoughts:

_____

_____

_____

_____

_____

How do I make them glad they came?

Date _____

This is the first step to a good meal for your customers!

Did the customer come in with a smile?_____

Did I greet my customers with a smile? _____

Did I give them their menu(s) when I seated them? _____

Were the specials discussed? _____

If yes, could I repeat them without looking?_____

Did I get their order correct? _____

Why or Why Not?_____

Did I check for condiments when I took their order?_____

How often and how many times did I stop at each table?_____

Were unnecessary trips made because I forgot something?

_____

Did I have to have help with my tables? _____ Why? _____

_____

Was I kind and courteous at all times?_____

_____

Did the customers leave with a smile?_____

What could I do differently?_____

_____

How I made them glad they came!

What did I learn today? _____

_____

How can I apply it tomorrow? _____

_____

What did I learn yesterday? _____

_____

Did I apply that today? _____

Who taught me something new today? _____

_____

Am I doing better than when I started? _____

_____

My Thoughts:

_____

_____

_____

_____

_____

_____

How do I make them glad they came?

Date _____

This is the first step to a good meal for your customers!

Did the customer come in with a smile?_____

Did I greet my customers with a smile? _____

Did I give them their menu(s) when I seated them? _____

Were the specials discussed? _____

If yes, could I repeat them without looking?_____

Did I get their order correct? _____

Why or Why Not?_____

Did I check for condiments when I took their order?_____

How often and how many times did I stop at each table?_____

Were unnecessary trips made because I forgot something?

_____

Did I have to have help with my tables? _____ Why? _____

_____

Was I kind and courteous at all times?_____

_____

Did the customers leave with a smile?_____

What could I do differently?_____

_____

How do I make them glad they came?

Date _____

This is the first step to a good meal for your customers!

Did the customer come in with a smile?_____

Did I greet my customers with a smile? _____

Did I give them their menu(s) when I seated them?
_____

Were the specials discussed? _____

If yes, could I repeat them without looking?_____

Did I get their order correct? _____

Why or Why Not?_____

Did I check for condiments when I took their order?_____

How often and how many times did I stop at each table?_____

Were unnecessary trips made because I forgot something?
_____

Did I have to have help with my tables? _____ Why? _____
_____

Was I kind and courteous at all times?_____
_____

Did the customers leave with a smile?_____

What could I do differently?_____

_____

How I made them glad they came!

What did I learn today? _____

_____

How can I apply it tomorrow? _____

_____

What did I learn yesterday?_____

_____

Did I apply that today? _____

Who taught me something new today?_____

_____

Am I doing better than when I started?_____

_____

My Thoughts:

_____

_____

_____

_____

_____

How do I make them glad they came?

Date _____

This is the first step to a good meal for your customers!

Did the customer come in with a smile?_____

Did I greet my customers with a smile? _____

Did I give them their menu(s) when I seated them?
_____

Were the specials discussed? _____

If yes, could I repeat them without looking? _____

Did I get their order correct? _____

Why or Why Not?_____

Did I check for condiments when I took their order?_____

How often and how many times did I stop at each table?_____

Were unnecessary trips made because I forgot something?

_____

Did I have to have help with my tables? _____ Why? _____

_____

Was I kind and courteous at all times?_____

_____

Did the customers leave with a smile?_____

What could I do differently?_____

_____

How I made them glad they came!

What did I learn today? _____

_____

How can I apply it tomorrow? _____

_____

What did I learn yesterday?_____

_____

Did I apply that today? _____

Who taught me something new today?_____

_____

Am I doing better than when I started?_____

_____

My Thoughts:

_____

_____

_____

_____

_____

_____

How do I make them glad they came?

Date _____

This is the first step to a good meal for your customers!

Did the customer come in with a smile?_____

Did I greet my customers with a smile? _____

Did I give them their menu(s) when I seated them?
_____

Were the specials discussed? _____

If yes, could I repeat them without looking? _____

Did I get their order correct? _____

Why or Why Not?_____

Did I check for condiments when I took their order?_____

How often and how many times did I stop at each table?_____

Were unnecessary trips made because I forgot something?
_____

Did I have to have help with my tables? _____ Why? _____
_____

Was I kind and courteous at all times?_____
_____

Did the customers leave with a smile?_____

What could I do differently?_____

_____

How I made them glad they came!

What did I learn today? _____

_____

How can I apply it tomorrow? _____

_____

What did I learn yesterday?_____

_____

Did I apply that today? _____

Who taught me something new today?_____

_____

Am I doing better than when I started?_____

_____

My Thoughts:

_____

_____

_____

_____

_____

_____

Thank you for buying this book!

If you enjoyed this book, please leave a positive review on Amazon.com

If you didn't enjoy this book, please email me at shyksos@gmail.com and let me know why!